Kim Van Gorp
Nancy Hoffman

Technology Editor
Jamie Wu Liu, M.A.

Project Manager
Paul Gardner

Editor-in-Chief
Sharon Coan, M.S. Ed.

Cover Designer
Lesley Palmer

Imaging
Ralph Olmedo, Jr.

Product Manager
Phil Garcia

Trademarks
QuickTime and the
QuickTime Logo are
trademarks used under license.

Publishers
Rachelle Cracchiolo, M.S. Ed.
Mary Dupuy Smith, M.S. Ed.

MULTIMEDIA
Collections

ROARING 20's & DEPRESSING 30's

I KNOW 3 TRADES
I SPEAK 3 LANGUAGES
FOUGHT FOR 3 YEARS
HAVE 3 CHILDREN
AND NO WORK FOR
3 MONTHS
BUT I ONLY WANT
ONE JOB

Authors

Paul Gardner and Jamie Wu Liu

Teacher Created Materials, Inc.
6421 Industry Way
Westminster, CA 92683
www.teachercreated.com
ISBN-0-7439-3039-8
©2002 Teacher Created Materials, Inc.
Made in U.S.A.

Table of Contents

Introduction

The following guide is provided to assist teachers and students as they prepare to use the photographs, clip art, audio clips, video clips, and documents presented on the multimedia CD. The images and clips provide effective resources that teachers and students can use to enhance presentations and projects.

For your convenience, thumbnail images of the photos and clip art that appear on the multimedia CD are included at the end of this section. They can be viewed in advance to decide which images to use for a particular project or lesson. A list of the audio clips, documents, and video clips is also included.

Whether used for a student's written report or multimedia presentation, to enhance an instructional lesson, or to stimulate students' critical thinking, you will discover that the resource materials on the multimedia CD will help enrich your learning experiences.

Technical Support

Phone: 1-800-858-7339

Email: custserv@teachercreated.com

Web Address: http://www.teachercreated.com/support

Acknowledgments

HyperStudio® is a registered trademark of Knowledge Adventure.

Print Shop® is a registered trademark of Mattel Interactive.

System Requirements

Requirements for Macintosh

- 32 MB RAM

- PowerMac/100 MHz or faster

- System 8.0 or later

- Color Monitor (1000s colors)

- QuickTime 4.0 (or later)*

- 4X CD-ROM (or faster)

Requirements for Windows

- 32 MB RAM

- 486/100 MHz or faster

- Windows 95/Windows 98

- Color Monitor (High Color-16 bit)

- QuickTime 4.0 (or later)*

- 4X CD-ROM (or faster)

QuickTime is available on the CD-ROM or can be downloaded from:
http://www.apple.com/quicktime See the ReadMe file for installation of *QuickTime* from the
CD-ROM. Make sure you choose "Full" or "Recommended" as the installation type.

Getting Started

Since the program runs directly from the CD-ROM, there is nothing to install. However, if you use an older computer or have adequate disk space, it is recommended that you copy the entire CD-ROM onto your hard drive so that it will run more efficiently.

> ***Macintosh Users:*** In some cases, the viewer program will not work correctly with *Adobe Type Manager* installed on Macintosh. If you are unable to see media in the program, it is recommended that the **ATM** control panel be turned off. To do this, open the **Extensions Manager** in the **Control Panels** folder in the **Apple** menu. Uncheck the **ATM** control panel, save the settings, and restart the computer.

Follow these instructions to run the program directly from the CD-ROM.

Macintosh Users

1. Insert the CD-ROM into the drive.

2. When the CD icon appears on the desktop, double-click the CD-ROM to open it.

3. Double-click the Player icon to start the program (Figure 1).

Figure 1

Figure 2

Windows Users

1. Insert the CD-ROM into the drive.

2. If the CD screen (Figure 1) does not appear, click on the Start menu and then the Run menu (Figure 2).

3. Click the Browse button and locate the CD-ROM.

4. Locate the Player.exe file and double-click to start the program.

If you see a message that says "This program requires *QuickTime* version 4.0 or later…," you need to install *QuickTime*. Click on the QuickTime Installer on this CD-ROM, or download *QuickTime* from *http://www.apple.com/quicktime*

Follow these instructions to copy the CD-ROM onto your hard drive and run the program from the hard drive.

Macintosh Users

1. Drag the entire CD-ROM icon to your hard drive.

2. When the CD-ROM icon appears on your hard drive, double-click it to open the CD-ROM.

3. Double-click the Player icon to start the program.

Windows Users

1. Copy the contents of the CD-ROM into a folder on your hard drive.

2. Locate the Player.exe file and double-click to start the program.

Using the Viewer Program

The Main Menu

This is the menu that appears after the program is started.

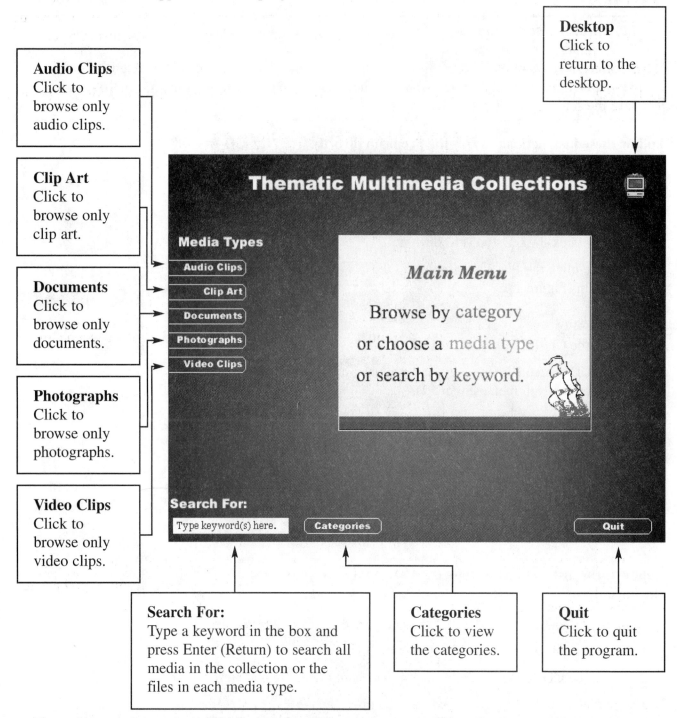

Audio Clips
Click to browse only audio clips.

Clip Art
Click to browse only clip art.

Documents
Click to browse only documents.

Photographs
Click to browse only photographs.

Video Clips
Click to browse only video clips.

Desktop
Click to return to the desktop.

Search For:
Type a keyword in the box and press Enter (Return) to search all media in the collection or the files in each media type.

Categories
Click to view the categories.

Quit
Click to quit the program.

Using the Viewer Program

The viewer program provided on the multimedia CD allows the user to easily access the media by either browsing or searching with keywords. The user can choose a media type (audio clips, clip art, documents, photographs, or video clips) and browse the files in that media, or the user can choose a category and browse the files by categories. By entering a keyword(s) or the first few letters of a word, a search can be done to find specific files in all of the media types or in one particular media type.

Browsing by Media Type

1. Click a media type button (**Audio Clips, Clip Art, Documents, Photographs,** or **Video Clips**) to view the list of files in that media type.

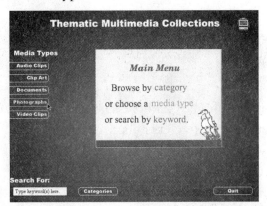

2. Click a file on the list to listen to the audio clip or look at the picture, document, or video clip.

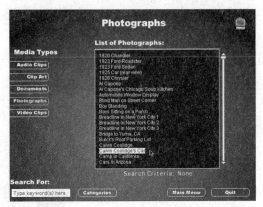

3. Click the **Back to List** button to return to the list. Click the **Right Arrow** to listen to the next audio clip or view the next picture, document, or video clip. Click the **Left Arrow** to go back to the previous item on the list.

Searching by Keyword

The user can search in all media types.

1. Click on the **Main Menu** button to go to the main menu if you are not already there.

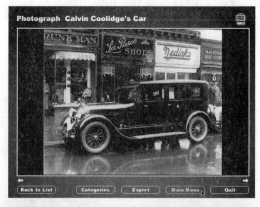

2. Type a keyword in the **Search For:** box and press **Enter (Return)** to view the list of search results. If no result is returned, try a different keyword. Typing in only the first few letters of a word gives the same result as when the entire word or a variation of this word is typed.

3. Click a file on the list to listen to the audio clip or look at the picture, document, or video clip.

4. Click the **Back to List** button to return to the list. Click the **Right Arrow** to listen to the next audio clip or view the next picture, document, or video clip. Click the **Left Arrow** to go back to the previous item on the list.

Using the Viewer Program

Searching by Keyword *(cont.)*

The user can also search in each media type.

1. Click the **Audio Clips** button.

2. Type a keyword in the **Search For:** box and press **Enter (Return).**

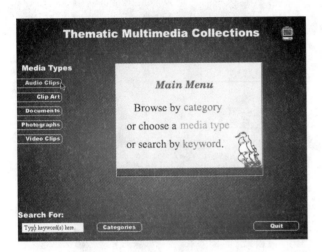

3. Click a file on the list of search results to select an audio clip (below left).

4. An audio control bar appears in the center of the screen (below right). Hold down the **Volume** key on the far left and scroll up or down to adjust the volume control. To listen to the audio clip, press the **Play** key (second from the left). Click on the **Rewind** key (second from the right) to rewind. The **Fast Forward** key is on the far right.

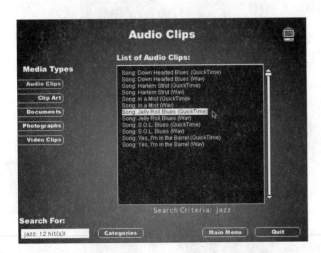

5. To search in another media type, click on the **Main Menu** button. Then, select that media type.

Browsing by Category

1. Click the **Categories** button to view the list of categories.

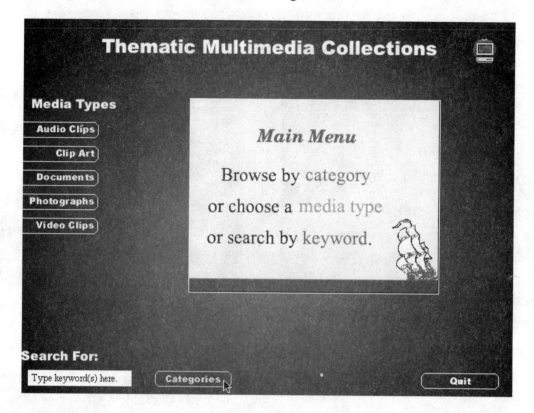

2. Click on a category title to view the files listed in that category.

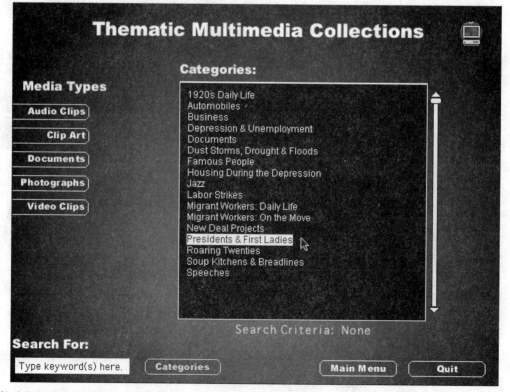

Browsing by Category *(cont.)*

3. Click a title to listen to the audio clip or look at the picture, document, or video clip.

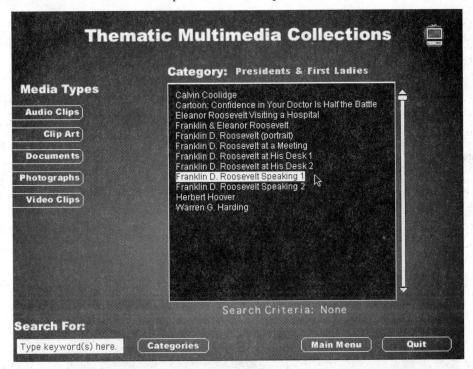

4. Click the **Back to List** button to return to the list. Click the **Right Arrow** to listen to the next audio clip or view the next picture, document, or video clip. Click the **Left Arrow** to go back to the previous item on the list.

5. Click the **Categories** button again and then click another category to view files in that category.

Using the Viewer Program

Copying and Pasting Photographs, Clip Art, and Text

The most efficient way to transfer photographs, clip art, and text from the viewer program into a document that you are working on is to copy and paste them. (*NOTE:* Audio and video files can be exported, but not copied and pasted; see pages 14 and 17.) Follow these easy steps to copy and paste.

1. Use the viewer to locate the photograph, clip art, or text that you want.

2. Click **Export** and choose **Copy to Clipboard**.

3. Click the **Desktop** button in the upper, right-hand corner to return to the computer's desktop.

4. If you have not already done so, open the document in which you wish to add the media.

5. Choose **Paste** from the **Edit** menu in the application that you are using to create the document. To add more pictures, return to the viewer program and repeat the process. The viewer program continues to run in the background until you click **Quit**.

   NOTE: Some applications, such as *Microsoft PowerPoint*, require that you choose **Paste Special** from the **Edit** menu and then select the option Bitmap (BMP) or Picture (PICT).

Copying and Pasting Photographs, Clip Art, and Text *(cont.)*

The viewer program provided on the multimedia CD also allows the user to easily save photograph or clip art files to several popular file formats, including BMP, EPS, GIF, JPEG, PICT, and TIFF. Follow these instructions to export files.

1. Click **Export** and choose **Save As**...

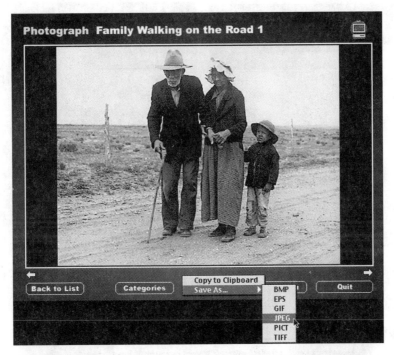

2. Choose the desired file format. (**GIF** export is not available on the Windows platform.)

3. Navigate to where you want to save the file (hard disk, floppy, etc.) and click **Save**.

Using the Viewer Program

Listening to and Exporting Audio Clips

Media Types: Click the **Audio Clips** button to view the list of audio clips (music, sound effects, etc.). Click any of the audio files listed to listen to them. These files have been provided in two formats: QuickTime and Wav. Consult your software documentation to find out which format works best for your application.

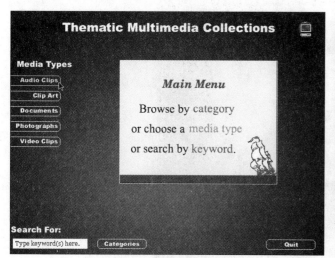

Search For: Type a keyword in the box here and press **Enter (Return)** to search only audio files.

Export: Click to export an audio clip for use in another program (see below). Navigate to where you want to save the file and click **Save**.

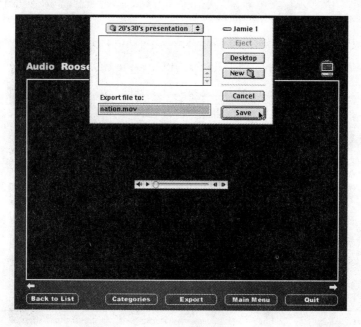

Back to List: Click to return to the list.

Arrows: Click the **Right Arrow** to go to the next audio clip and the **Left Arrow** to go to the previous one on the list.

Main Menu: Click to return to the main menu.

Using the Viewer Program

Viewing and Exporting Clip Art and Photographs

Media Types: Click the **Clip Art** or **Photographs** button to view the list of files. Click any of the clip art or photograph files listed to preview them.

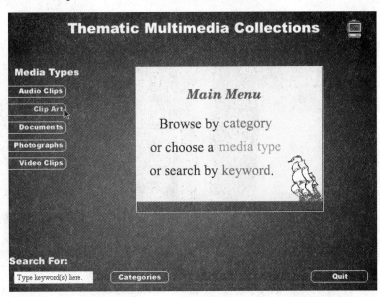

Search For: Type a keyword and press **Enter (Return)** to search only files in that media type.

Export: Click to export the image for use in another program. Choose **Copy to Clipboard** to copy and paste the image into another program, or choose **Save As...** and a file type to export the image for use in another program. (**GIF** export is not available on the Windows platform.) *NOTE:* Some applications, such as *Microsoft PowerPoint*, require that you choose **Paste Special** from the **Edit** menu and then select the option Bitmap (BMP) or Picture (PICT).

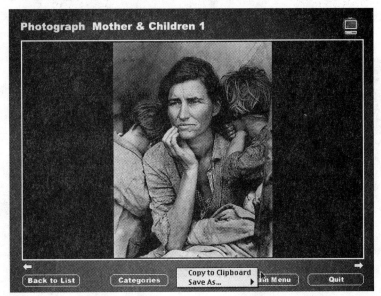

Back to List: Click to return to the list.

Arrows: Click the **Right Arrow** to see the next picture and the **Left Arrow** to go to the previous one on the list.

Main Menu: Click to return to the main menu.

Viewing and Exporting Documents

Media Types: Click the **Documents** button to view the list of documents. Click any of the files listed to preview the document.

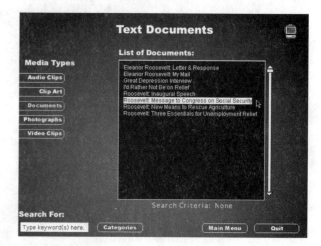

Search For: Type a keyword in the box and press **Enter (Return)** to search only the text documents.

Export: Click to export the text for use in another program. Choose **Export Text File** (below left) to copy the entire text of a document. Navigate to where you want to save the file and click **Save.**

Or, choose **Copy Selection to Clipboard** (below right) to copy and paste part of the text into another program. To select only part of the text, hold down the mouse button and highlight the desired text.

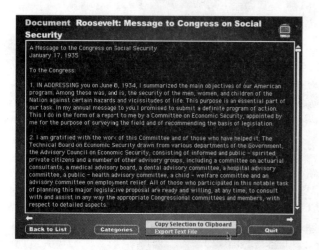

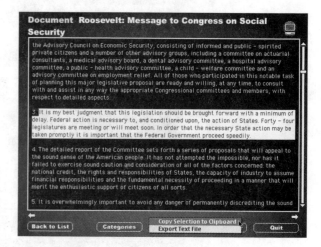

Back to List: Click to return to the list of documents.

Arrows: Click the **Right Arrow** to see the next document and the **Left Arrow** to go to the previous one on the list.

Main Menu: Click to return to the main menu.

Using the Viewer Program

Viewing and Exporting Video Clips

Media Types: Click the **Video Clips** button to view the list of video clips. Click any of the video files listed to preview them. Video clips are provided in both QuickTime and AVI formats. Consult your software documentation to find out which format works best for your application. On the Windows platform, AVIs are the most compatible with *PowerPoint*.

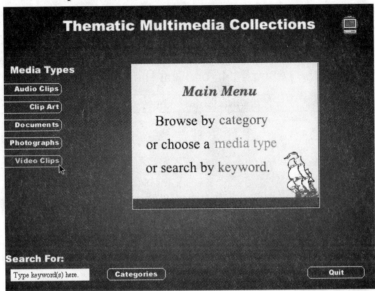

Search For: Type a keyword in the box and press **Enter (Return)** to search only video files.

Export: Click to export the video clip for use in another program. Navigate to where you want to save the file, and click **Save**.

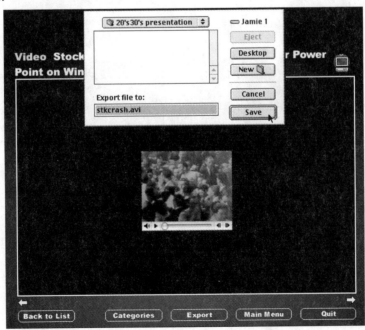

Back to List: Click to return to the list.

Arrows: Click the **Right Arrow** to see the next video and the **Left Arrow** to go to the previous one on the list.

Main Menu: Click to return to the main menu.

Ideas for Using Multimedia Collections in the Classroom

Teacher Uses

- Insert a series of photographs in a word-processing document and insert notes or captions. Print these on an overhead transparency and use them as visual aids.

- Use photos of people, places, and things as flashcards for students to study. For younger students, have them simply identify the photos. With older students, you can use the flashcards to have them identify the significance of the photographs.

- Import photos into a word-processing document to illustrate student work sheets. Have students explain the importance of the person, item, or event shown in the photos.

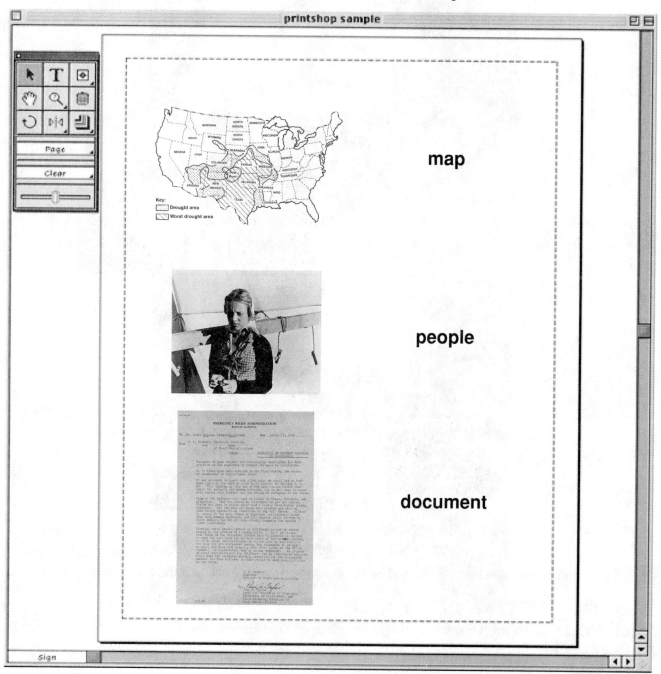

Ideas for Using Multimedia Collections in the Classroom

Teacher Uses *(cont.)*

- Create interactive practice activities using multimedia software such as *HyperStudio*.

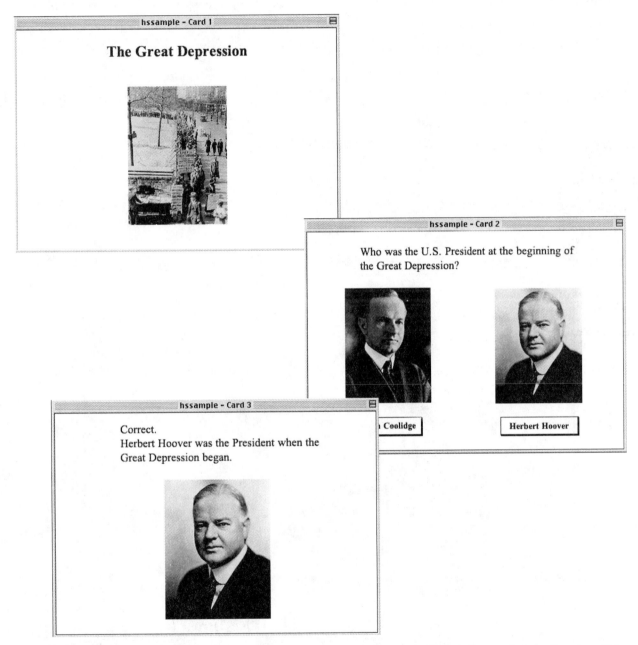

- Import a series of images into slide-show software such as *Microsoft PowerPoint*. Set the slide show to repeat itself on a computer at the front of the classroom or on a connected TV monitor. Use this simple slide show to grab students' attention as they walk into the classroom.

- Create a multimedia presentation using images and sound or video to illustrate your lesson.

- Make a Web page activity using the images and adding any hypertext links to sites you want your students to visit. Save the Web page to a folder on your hard drive so students can view it quickly. Include sounds or video clips to add more interest.

Ideas for Using Multimedia Collections in the Classroom

Teacher Uses *(cont.)*

- Open a video file in your Web browser for students to use at a learning center in your classroom. Provide students with several questions to answer about the images they see. You could also create a Web page with the questions and video file on one screen.

  NOTE: The HTML code for embedding a *QuickTime* movie file in a Web page is

  <embed src="file:///drive/folder/file" width="320" height="255" autoplay="true">

  where width is the width in pixels of the actual movie and height is the movie height plus about 15 pixels for the *QuickTime* bar at the bottom of the movie. The file location would be wherever you have saved it on your computer's hard drive.

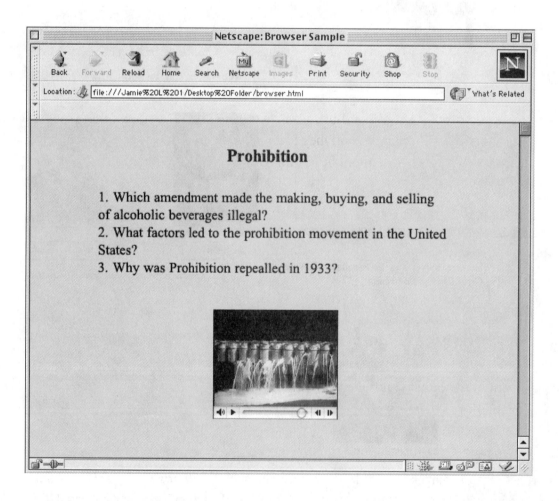

- Print a photo using word-processing or sign-making software, then use it as a bulletin board weekly challenge. Have a "suggestion box" under the photo and let students write their names and guesses on paper, then insert them in the box. Use that same image as part of a lesson once you have pulled all the entries out of the box. Award a monthly prize to the students with the most correct guesses. Create a certificate using all four of that month's challenge photos.

Ideas for Using Multimedia Collections in the Classroom

Student Uses

- Have students create diagrams by importing photos or clip art into a paint or draw program. Use the line and text tools to label parts or call attention to details.

- Students can import the images and other files into multimedia presentations rather than writing typical reports about the topic.

- Have students make posters about the people, places, and events of a particular time period. They can import a photo into word-processing or sign-making software such as *Microsoft® Works*, *AppleWorks* (formerly known as *ClarisWorks*), or *Print Shop*. Once they have researched the subject in the photo, they can create their posters and include important pieces of information.

- Students can make period newspapers. Have them use newsletter-making software or word-processing software to create newspapers for the time period they are studying. They can then import the photos or clip-art images to illustrate their articles.

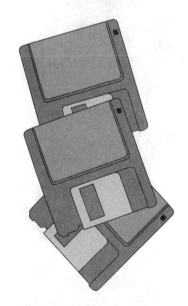

- Let teams of students create challenges for each other. Have them use simple photo-editing software to add special effects to portraits of famous people in order to stump the opposing teams as they try to guess who the people are.

- Students can create multimedia presentations based on various songs included in the sound files. They can find the lyrics to the songs and use them as the headings on slides, adding photos that help illustrate the songs.

- Have student teams create multimedia presentations for a special technology parent night. Have them use the image, video, and sound files to create *HyperStudio* (or other multimedia program) presentations about what they have learned during their study of a particular topic. If you have a computer lab, have the students save their projects to various computers around the room. If you don't have a lab, try to get a projector or television connector so you can show the program to the entire classroom. Invite parents to come and have the students show off their presentations. You might want to invite the principal and board of education members to this event as well.

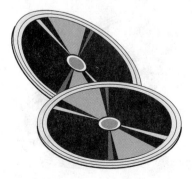

Student Uses *(cont.)*

- Students can write stories based on particular images. Have them import the images at the top of a word-processing document and then write about what is happening.

- Assign topics to the students and have them write research papers and import several images to help illustrate the topic. This is a great way to practice their word-processing skills.

- Have groups of students create multimedia presentations to "teach the class" about a concept you are studying. Each group in the class can have a different concept. They can use the image, sound, and video files in their multimedia presentations. You can keep these presentations on your classroom computer for students to use as review before tests.

- Have students create slide shows using *PowerPoint*, *HyperStudio*, or another multimedia program, adding their own narration rather than entering text into each slide. This may take some planning in order to find a quiet place in your room or a computer lab area for them to do the recording.

- Students could also present the "Morning News" in your classroom, using news clips from the time period you are studying. They could use the images and video files to represent the "filmed event" they are reporting. Videotape the students reporting the news with the computer monitor sitting behind them and facing toward the audience (and video camera).

- At the end of the year, have students create a multimedia presentation on "What We Learned This Year" to present to the next year's class. They could incorporate previous multimedia presentations or start from scratch and create a new project.

Ideas for Presenting Projects

One of the main purposes of multimedia presentations is to report information to others. After a project is created, it still needs to be presented. Presenting projects to the entire class enables the students to learn from one another. Presenting gives students the chance to brag about something they may have discovered. This is also a good opportunity for students to share difficulties they may have had with technical components of the project. There are many ways students can share their projects with others.

Oral Reporting

Let students stand up in front of the class to present their multimedia creations. Many projects are perfect for display on a television screen. Students can explain what they learned while displaying the cards or slides that they created. Let the students be in charge of the presentations. You may even want to incorporate a presentation component into the assessment of the project.

Video Reporting

Students (especially those who are shy about public speaking) may want to record their presentations onto video tape. They can then show the video-taped projects to an audience and follow each with a question-and-answer period.

Disk Exchange

Students may want to copy the contents of their multimedia projects onto disks for other classrooms to view. This gives students from different classrooms and grade levels an opportunity to see what your students have learned.

Using a Wide Screen Projection Device

By using a wide screen projection device, projects can easily be presented to the entire class. Many converters are available to fit a variety of different computers. Contact your local computer supply store or mail order catalog to purchase these. The addition of a VCR to this set up allows you to print multimedia projects to tape. To print to tape, insert a blank tape into the VCR and press record before the students begin. The diagram below shows how audio and video can be presented on a television.

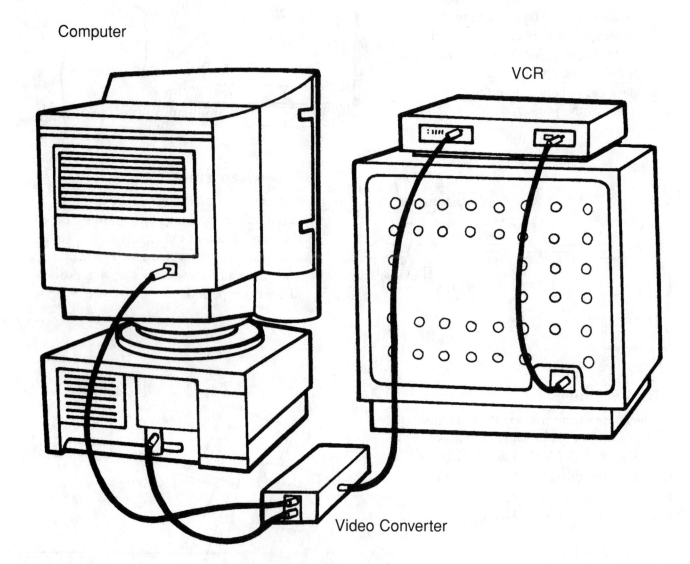

Computer

VCR

Video Converter

Creating Class Web Pages

Another exciting way to present your classroom's multimedia projects is to create your own Web page.

You will need to follow these steps:

1. Gather information.

2. Determine your intended audience.

3. Create a storyboard.

4. Plan your navigational tools.

5. Create an aesthetically appealing Web page.

Designing Web Pages

When designing your page, keep the following ideas in mind.

Format

The format should be user friendly. Your page should have a clear scope, be easy to understand and use, and include appropriate, clearly labeled links.

Aesthetic Appeal

Graphics should be able to be quickly downloaded and be relevant to the page. Text should be easy to read. The background should be subdued and coordinate with text colors and graphics. Remember to creatively use graphics and colors.

Content

The content needs to be credible. Information must be accurate and complete.

Learning Process

The page should challenge learners to think, reflect, discuss, hypothesize, compare, classify, etc.

Engaging

The Web page should engage the learner.

Suggested Software for Creating Web Pages

Web WorkShop (Sunburst)

Thumbnail Photo Images and Clip Art

chandler.jpg

1920 Chandler

roadster.jpg

1923 Ford Roadster

sedan.jpg

1923 Ford Sedan

carrear.jpg

1925 Car (rear view)

sedan2.jpg

1926 Nash Sedan

chrysler.jpg

1928 Chrysler

alcapone.jpg

Al Capone

soup3.jpg

Al Capone's Chicago
Soup Kitchen

carwindo.jpg

Automobile Window
Display

Thumbnail Photo Images and Clip Art

man3.jpg

Blind Man on
Street Corner

boystand.jpg

Boy Standing

children.jpg

Boys Sitting on a Porch

bread1.jpg

Breadline in New York
City 1

bread2.jpg

Breadline in New York
City 2

bread3.jpg

Breadline in New York
City 3

yuma.jpg

Bridge to Yuma, CA

roofpark.jpg

Buick's Roof Parking Lot

coolidge.jpg

Calvin Coolidge

Thumbnail Photo Images and Clip Art

coolcar.jpg

Calvin Coolidge's Car

camp.jpg

Camp in California

cars.jpg

Cars in Arizona

parklot.jpg

Cars in Parking Lot

onroad9.jpg

Cars on the Road:
Looking for Work

doctor.jpg

Cartoon: Confidence in
Your Doctor Is Half the
Battle

lindber2.jpg

Charles Lindbergh (1927)

lindberg.jpg

Charles Lindbergh & the
Spirit of St. Louis

doorway2.jpg

Child & Father Standing
in Doorway

Thumbnail Photo Images and Clip Art

kidtire.jpg

Child Sitting on a Tire

doorway1.jpg

Child Standing in
Doorway

kids.jpg

Children Sitting in a
Field

clothing.jpg

Clothing Store

couple.jpg

Couple & Automobile
Silhouette

cards2.jpg

Couple Playing Cards

dancing.jpg

Couples Dancing at
Hotel

crop.jpg

Drought-Stricken Crops

codust.jpg

Dust Storm in Colorado

Thumbnail Photo Images and Clip Art

ksdust.jpg

Dust Storm in Kansas

sddust.jpg

Dust Storm in
South Dakota

dustst.jpg

Dust Storm in Town

txdust.jpg

Dust Storm in Texas

dustfarm.jpg

Dust Storm on a Farm

anderson.jpg

Eleanor Roosevelt
Awards Marian Anderson
the Spingarn Medal

eleanor.jpg

Eleanor Roosevelt
Visiting a Hospital

migrate1.jpg

Emergency Relief
Administration
Document

looking1.jpg

Employment Agency 1

looking2.jpg

Employment Agency 2

family4.jpg

Family Eating
Christmas Dinner

family2.jpg

Family in Doorway

family1.jpg

Family in Front of
Shack 1

infront4.jpg

Family in Front of
Shack 2

family3.jpg

Family in Home

kitchen.jpg

Family in Tenement
Kitchen

tent.jpg

Family Standing by Tent

walking3.jpg

Family Walking on the
Road 1

Thumbnail Photo Images and Clip Art

walking4.jpg

Family Walking on the
Road 2

farm.jpg

Farm Forclosure

forsale1.jpg

Farm Foreclosure
"For Sale" Sign 1

forsale2.jpg

Farm Foreclosure
"For Sale" Sign 2

forsale3.jpg

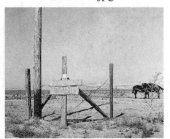

Farm Foreclosure
"For Sale" Sign 3

dtrelief.jpg

Farmers Applying for
Drought Relief

flood1.jpg

Farmyard Covered with
Flood Waters 1

flood2.jpg

Farmyard Covered with
Flood Waters 2

girlad.jpg

Fashion: Girls' Clothing
Advertisement

Thumbnail Photo Images and Clip Art

hats.jpg

Fashion: Hat Display

bathsuit.jpg

Fashion: Bathing Suit
Advertisement

stocking.jpg

Fashion: Stocking
Advertisement

womenfur.jpg

Fashion: Women
Wearing Furs

fashion1.jpg

Fashion: Women's
Clothing Advertisement 1

fashion2.jpg

Fashion: Women's
Clothing Advertisement 2

fashion3.jpg

Fashion: Women's
Clothing Advertisement 3

fashion4.jpg

Fashion: Women's
Clothing Advertisement 4

flapper2.jpg

Flapper

Thumbnail Photo Images and Clip Art

flood3.jpg

Flood Refugees in
Arkansas 1

flood4.jpg

Flood Refugees in
Arkansas 2

fdrmtg.jpg

Franklin D. Roosevelt at
a Meeting

fdrseat1.jpg

Franklin D. Roosevelt at
His Desk 1

fdrseat3.jpg

Franklin D. Roosevelt at
His Desk 2

fdrport1.jpg

Franklin D. Roosevelt
(portrait)

fdrtalk1.jpg

Franklin D. Roosevelt
Speaking 1

fdrtalk2.jpg

Franklin D. Roosevelt
Speaking 2

roosevel.jpg

Franklin & Eleanor
Roosevelt

Thumbnail Photo Images and Clip Art

furnitur.jpg

Furniture Store

radio4.jpg

Girl Listening to Radio

girl.jpg

Girl Standing
in Front of a Tent

hoover1.jpg

Herbert Hoover

shack.jpg

Homes During the
Depression

hotel.jpg

Hotel Left Unfinished
During Great Depression

industry.jpg

Industry Montage

mnstrike.jpg

Labor Strike in
Minneapolis

nystrike.jpg

Labor Strike in
New York 1

Thumbnail Photo Images and Clip Art

strikeny.jpg

Labor Strike in
New York 2

sfstrike.jpg

Labor Strike in
San Francisco

dcstrike.jpg

Labor Strike in
Washington, DC

infront1.jpg

Man & Boy
in Front of Shack

sit1.jpg

Man & Boy Sitting

cards.jpg

Man Dealing Cards

dustman.jpg

Man in Dust Storm

man1.jpg

Man Leaning Against
Vacant Store

mansit.jpg

Man Sitting
in Front of Shack

Thumbnail Photo Images and Clip Art

mansit1.jpg

Man Sitting on Step

manstand.jpg

Man Standing on Road

man2.jpg

Man Walking

walking1.jpg

Man Walking
on the Road

dustmap.jpg

Map: Dust Bowl

looking3.jpg

Men Registering for Jobs

mansit3.jpg

Men Sitting on Corner

rowofmen.jpg

Men Sitting on Curb

onfarm2.jpg

Men Working on a Farm

mother1.jpg

Mother & Children 1

mother2.jpg

Mother & Children 2

mother3.jpg

Mother & Children 3

mother4.jpg

Mother & Children 4

family5.jpg

Mother & Her Children

sit2.jpg

Mother & Her
Children Sitting

mother18.jpg

Mother Sitting by Tent
with Child

stockex.jpg

New York Stock
Exchange

onroadnm.jpg

On the Road in
New Mexico

Thumbnail Photo Images and Clip Art

onroadok.jpg

On the Road in
Oklahoma

onroadtx.jpg

On the Road in Texas

onroad1.jpg

On the Road to
California 1

onroad2.jpg

On the Road to
California 2

onroad3.jpg

On the Road to
California 3

onroad4.jpg

On the Road to
California 4

onroad5.jpg

On the Road to
California 5

onroad6.jpg

On the Road to
California 6

onroad7.jpg

On the Road to
California 7

Thumbnail Photo Images and Clip Art

onroad8.jpg

On the Road to
California 8

standing.jpg

People Standing in
Doorway

checks.jpg

People Waiting for
Relief Checks

bank.jpg

People Waiting
Outside a Bank

walking2.jpg

People Walking
Down a Road

mural1.jpg

Public Works Artist
Painting a Mural

mural2.jpg

Public Works Artists
Painting a Mural

wpabridg.jpg

Public Works Bridge

worker.jpg

Public Works
Construction Workers

dam.jpg

Public Works
Dam in Oregon

electric.jpg

Public Works
Electrical Training

workgirl.jpg

Public Works Lithograph:
Working Girls Going
Home

village.jpg

Public Works Mural:
Fishermen's Village

history.jpg

Public Works Mural:
History of
Southern Illinois

mural.jpg

Public Works Mural:
Hyde Park Scenes

wpa3.jpg

Public Works
Musicians Entertaining
Flood Victims

nya.jpg

Public Works Painting of
National Youth
Administration

newdeal.jpg

Public Works Painting:
The New Deal

Thumbnail Photo Images and Clip Art

winter.jpg

Public Works Painting:
Winter Scenes

dustyear.jpg

Public Works Poster:
Years of Dust

wpa1.jpg

Public Works Project:
Building Statue

sew.jpg

Public Works
Sewing Shop

play.jpg

Public Works
Theater Show:
Horse Eat Hat

typing.jpg

Public Works
Typing Class

radio2.jpg

Radio Broadcasters

radio3.jpg

Radio Coil Winder

radio.jpg

Radio Inspector

Thumbnail Photo Images and Clip Art

mail.jpg

Radio Station Fan Mail

intfridg.jpg

Refrigerator
Advertisement 1

adfridge.jpg

Refrigerator
Advertisement 2

relief2.jpg

Rural Relief Station 1

relief1.jpg

Rural Relief Station 2

school2.jpg

School Classroom in
Alabama

school1.jpg

School Classroom in
Tennessee

service1.jpg

Service Station 1

service2.jpg

Service Station 2

Thumbnail Photo Images and Clip Art

shackal.jpg

Shack in Alabama

shackca1.jpg

Shack in California 1

shackca2.jpg

Shack in California 2

shackca4.jpg

Shack in California 3

shackil.jpg

Shack in Illinois

shackia.jpg

Shack in Iowa

shacktn.jpg

Shack in Tennessee

shacks.jpg

Shacks Along a River in Portland

soil2.jpg

Soil Drifts on a Farm

Thumbnail Photo Images and Clip Art

soil.jpg

Soil Erosion

squat1.jpg

Squatters Along a
California Highway 1

squat2.jpg

Squatters Along a
California Highway 2

crash.jpg

Stock Market Crash
(Black Thursday, 1929)

29graph.jpg

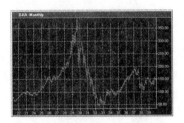

Stock Market Crash
(graph)

nyc.jpg

Street in New York City

town.jpg

Street in Oklahoma Town

rail1.jpg

Strikers at Burlington
Railroad Shop Yards 1

rail3.jpg

Strikers at Burlington
Railroad Shop Yards 2

Thumbnail Photo Images and Clip Art

soup1.jpg

Unemployed Man
Eating Soup

manlying.jpg

Unemployed Man
Lying on Curb

march.jpg

Unemployed March in
New York City

men.jpg

Unemployed Men

soup4.jpg

Unemployed Men
Eating Soup

soup2.jpg

Unemployed Men
Lined up at
Soup Kitchen

camp2.jpg

Unemployed
Women's Camp

vacuum.jpg

Vacuum Cleaner Display

wallst.jpg

Wall Street

Thumbnail Photo Images and Clip Art

harding1.jpg

Warren G. Harding

washmach.jpg

Washing Machine
Advertisement

washing.jpg

Washing Machine
Display

infront3.jpg

Woman & Child
in Front of Home

workkitc.jpg

Woman in Camp Kitchen

woman.jpg

Woman Smiling

washing2.jpg

Woman with Washbasin

exercise.jpg

Women in School
Exercise Uniforms

workwash.jpg

Workers Washing

Audio Clips, Video Clips, and Documents

Audio Clips

Songs

Down Hearted Blues

Harlem Strut

In a Mist

Jelly Roll Blues

S.O.L. Blues

Yes, I'm in the Barrel

Speeches by Franklin D. Roosevelt

Inaugural Oath

Inaugural Speech Excerpt

New Deal

One Third of a Nation

Revive & Prospe

Video Clips

harles Lindbergh in Airplane

Feeding People During Great Depression

Flappers Fashion Show

Refrigerator Theater Commercial

Stock Market Crash of 1929

Stock Market Traders

Transporting Liquor During Prohibition

Documents

Eleanor Roosevelt: Letter & Response

Eleanor Roosevelt: My Mail

Great Depression Interview

I'd Rather Not Be on Relief

FDR: Inaugural Speech

FDR: Message to Congress on Social Security

FDR: New Means to Rescue Agriculture

FDR: Three Essentials for Unemployment Relief